SPLIT SECONDS

How to be enlightened while remaining neurotic

BHARAT ROCHLIN

HERE *and* NOW DREAM PUBLISHING

TIRUVANNAMALAI

i

This Edition Published in India by

Here And Now Dream Publishing.

Tiruvannamalai, India

www.ombharat.com

© Bharat Rochlin 1997

Cover Design By Dream Designs

Cover Illustration By Bharat

Designed And Typeset By Dream Designs

India Library Cataloguing in Publication data available

Library Of Congress Cataloguing in Publication data

Available

ISBN 978-81-90627-3-20

CONTENTS

AUTHOR'S NOTE

This urge: to express the inexpressible came during the course of my meetings with Shree HWL Poonjaji, known as Papaji - he inspired me to write this narrative.

Papaji's total love of truth and the immensity of joy he showed when someone got 'it' and could say something about it also filled my heart with the song of truth and the urge to express it.

As the book developed, I discovered I was presenting myself and sharing my story not as a teacher, but as a fellow being who experienced awakening and recognizes his merging into this mystery. This book is not intended to be biographical.

I hope in some way this narrative touches the truth of your being, that you recognize that enlightenment is not only real but possible, and that it is available now, perhaps more so than ever before. No longer is enlightenment obtainable only to a select few who win it after some long and arduous journey. Enlightenment can happen to you or me as simply as being here now.

This story revolves around seven episodes called 'Split Seconds', which represent moments when time disappears, truth is revealed and transformation occurs. These moments are usually of the ultimate experience, changing the person profoundly.

I am not an expert on the meaning of existence, but I know it is a mystery I am part of, and yet, it is beyond me.

It is not possible to understand the mystery of awakening; however, it appears that for every being that has experienced self-realization, there are that many ways the mystery wants someone to flower - there are no rules and nothing is fixed.

Enlightenment is real and possible and worth anything to have. The joy of awakening is so immense, that the awaken one wants to scream on the rooftop for others to hear and know, and realize themselves.

The pot at the end of the rainbow does exist and it is filled with peace and love, wholeness and well-being.

you are just there

no future
no past
a table is a table
a chair a chair

just being

all is being

INTRODUCTION

Once people truly believed the sun revolved around the earth. Standing here on earth, this belief certainly appears to be true. When Copernicus proclaimed the truth that the earth revolves around the sun, he was not believed and was persecuted as well. When Sages (Wisemen) proclaim we are not the body and personality but something greater, they are not believed either. After all, the body and personality are so close and recognizable as us, and from this viewpoint this perception certainly appears to be true.

The fact is truth is not always obvious. What appears to be real is not always the case and we are often fooled by the apparent logic and the narrowness of the perception of mind.

Split seconds are defined as moments when mind disappears and reality is perceived without distortion. This lifting of the veil of illusion is one aspect of enlightenment and is analogous to waking up from normal sleep to everyday consciousness.

When awakening occurs, for example, through the experience of a split second as described above, one begins to understand that Truth exists. Now it is understood that something beyond the perceptions of mind is present. Usually this wakefulness has a short duration and sleep returns. The knowing becomes an experience, a memory; yet something remains that drives the experiencer to search for it again. In this way, a conscious desire for truth arises. The intrinsic longing for truth has always been there but now the experiencer consciously knows it. As more veils of illusion disappear and also when there is reoccurrence of illusions, the desire to remain in truth becomes of paramount importance, a matter of life and death. For the awakened person, there is nothing more important than to continue to dive deeper and deeper into the divine mystery.

Chapter 1

BIRTH

Goa, India, 1975.

After living in Europe a few years, I decided to travel overland to Goa. A friend told me there were dancing girls on the beach and in Goa there existed a alternative free society where the normal social rules were not adhered to. Upon arrival, after three months of travel, I found this all to be true and even beyond my expectations. There were beautiful girls dancing naked on the beach and I could be exactly as I wanted.

I built a bamboo hut on Anjuna beach and settled in with my girl-friend. We went to innumerable parties and met many crazy and outra-geous people doing their best to be crazy and outrageous. I never felt so free. I could let go of my inhibitions and allow myself among other things to wear exotic clothes and use make-up.

After awhile though, 1 lost interest in parties and being in the scene. I became quiet and stayed mostly around my hut cooking and watching glorious sunsets every evening.

There lived in the hut next to us a couple who were different from people we were used to meeting. The man was Swiss and had been living in India for seven years. Everyday I watched him do exercises and move his body into crazy postures, sometimes remaining for hours in the same position. Somebody told me he was practicing something called Yoga.

His American girlfriend was around eight or nine months pregnant. She told me one day she was planning to have the baby in her hut without a doctor. 'I am trusting in existence', she explained. This was the first time ever I heard this expression. I found it hard to believe; coming from New York City it was almost inconceivable. I thought she was either crazy or really stupid.

Finally the day arrived. It was a beautiful and sunny afternoon. There was a slight breeze coming from the sea and it soothed our hot skins. Four of us were present in her hut preparing for the baby's arrival. I did not suspect or imagine that on this day I would meet with truth.

SPLIT SECONDS 1

There was a childbirth one day.
It was in an unusual location by the sea.
There within a bamboo hut,
I became immersed in a sharing
that brought to light the luminosity,
which had always been but was as yet unseen, unfelt.
We were there helping, watching in awe,
this mystery of childbearing. All the more so
since nobody really knew what to do.
Time seemed to stop.
The air stood still...   heavy...   and thick.
We were lost in the contractions,
the rise and fall of her breath,
as if nothing else seemed to exist.
Slowly, slowly, the baby appeared,
first the head and finally the feet
until at last he was out and free.
In that moment or some moment

I know not which,
as if a hurricane wind swept through the hut,
a Presence, an Energy, an Intelligence
or God if you will,
was there, knocking us off our feet.
We weeped,
we rejoiced,
we held each other dear,
for so magnificent was its presence,
so absolute was its feeling.
In this moment of Birth,
of Truth, of Beauty,
a conscious determination to know, arose.

Chapter 2

DIVINE DESCENT

The sun was sinking into the ocean as I returned to my hut. My friend was busy cooking over a wood fire. I sat close and shared with her what had happened. I told her I must find out what meditation and yoga are about - whatever happened, tasted so good, I wanted it again.

In this way I became conscious of my desire for God. I did not do anything for it; it came to me and gave me my purpose.

Soon it was time to leave Goa. We decided to travel by sea to Bombay. While passing the beaches of Goa on the ferry, I felt a immense rush of bliss.

'Thank you Goa, you have been so good to me."

From Bombay we traveled to New Delhi. In New Delhi, my friend and I parted ways and I traveled by train to Benares to buy a sitar.

Waiting at the Delhi train station, I experienced a level of energy as never before. I felt so high and free, and just totally wonderful.

While in Delhi, I bought a book called *Raja Yoga*. In this book, the author described the seven bodies we consist of, starting from the physical body and ending with the spiritual body called the Supreme Self or Atma.

He suggested a technique to realize the Atma by rejecting everything you can see about yourself as not the self. Continue rejecting until nothing is left. In this way you will reach to the Supreme Self.

I practiced this in Benares and some understanding arose that I am that, The Supreme Self.

I was feeling so beautiful inside, a feeling of something new and wonderful about to happen. It was in the air. I wanted only to be good so I could be with God.

In Benares, I met a Spanish man studying sitar named Fernando Diaz. I stayed in his house and began to feel a most loving connection with him.

It was during my stay with Fernando that the window to the divine opened again.

SPLIT SECOND 2

The holy city Benares,
that frontier between worlds,
of burning ghats and Mother Ganga embraced me
one evening while walking with a friend.
A man suddenly appeared out of the teeming
masses surrounding us,
touched my forehead and disappeared.
"Why did he do that?"I wondered.
"You have been blessed,"
my friend answered.
Later at home we shared our food
and music.
So perfect was this warm night.
I stepped out onto the veranda for some air.
I saw in the distant many fires and heard chaotic
drumming coming from several marriage ceremonies. While
standing there, suddenly, the sky seemed to light up and open.

*Everything stood still as if I was in a vacuum and
not of this world.
An immense feeling but more
than a feeling, closer to a Presence, overwhelmed me that
God was there.
God was there and was surrounding me,
surrounding the Universe.
God was there and only its presence was felt.
In this total immensity I bathed,
merging with its glory,
until a feeling occurred, that if God is here,
he is coming for me and I will die.
My body and being quivered in fear as I fell apart.
It was then left to my friend to soothe my heart.*

Chapter 3

THE MIRACLE OF DELHI

The experience in Benares touched me deeply. When God descended and I experienced the immense fear of dying, it seemed more real than real. I thought for sure I would die. Later, when I recovered and was still alive, it was obvious that the feeling, which seemed so real, was not real. From this experience I discovered that the world, as I perceived it, as real as it seems, was not necessarily true or correct.

After spending a delightful day choosing a sitar, I left Benares for New Delhi. I purchased a sitar case there and booked a train ticket to Pakistan because my visa was due to expire in a few days. The train was scheduled to leave in the evening so I spent the day shopping at Connaught Place. I entered a market building to purchase peanut butter and crackers for the trip.

Upon leaving the building I stepped into the next Split Second and perhaps the grandest moment of my life.

SPLIT SECOND 3

It is a day in New Delhi.
At Connaught Place, the streets and shops are full with the
noise and bustle of countless people going to and fro,
as only in India it can be.
I am there within the chaos.
I walk out of a building and spy a man
leaning against a wall.
When I look at him,
something occurs, which never happened before.
I am deeply touched within
and my heart leaps out exploding in love.
Thinking he's a beggar, I offer him some money.
While doing this, he grabs my arm
and looks intensely into my eyes.
I immediately sense that he is not a beggar
but a Holyman.

We look at each other for awhile.
Some words are spoken but neither of us can understand. After
some time, he makes a signal with his hands
and I understand he wants me to go with him. I somehow
convey
in the same fashion, I will go with him, but first, I want to
return to my hotel to drop off my shopping.
Feeling he understands me, I leave.
At the hotel, I ponder over whether to return.
I sense meeting this man
will change my life forever.
It feels as scary as if jumping off a cliff. Nevertheless, I know I
must go; there is no choice.
I am glad he is there when I return.
He smiles and motions for me to follow.
We walk together in silence onto a narrow side street. Immedi-
ately we are away from the
crowds
and noise. On the right side I notice
a small park.
We walk around the corner following its outer perimeter.
While we are walking, I begin to be aware that
he is talking to me and I understand him.
I listen for some time until it dawns on me that his voice is not
coming from his lips (they are not moving), but rather I hear his
voice inside my brain. Astonishingly I realize he is talking to me

through telepathy.
I can hardly believe this is happening,
yet it is. He begins to tell me everything about myself
and what will be in the future.
Meanwhile, I notice I am feeling very good.
Something very special is happening.
And all that seems to exist: is this man,
his voice in my brain and walking down the street.
We approach a gate and enter into the park that contains one
fairly large tree surrounded by a grassy area. We approach the
tree and to my surprise, another man joins us,
and they start talking.
Looking over beyond the fence,
I see a man with a painted cow that strikes me as unusual. He
seems to have a connection also
with what is going on.
The amazing thing is, I feel no fear
being together with these strange men.
Looking closer at the other man,
I notice he looks unusual.
The skin of his face seems shaped with plastic putty
and he has the biggest and most curved hooknose
I've ever seen. He seems to have an actor's face.
The three of us sit under the tree, Hooknose to my left
and Holyman to my right.
After some time Hooknose begins to make some unusual

sounds
and moves his lips in such a strange way,
it would be very difficult to repeat.
These sounds have an affect
because I notice we have become relaxed. As he continues to
emit these sounds,
we get even more relaxed and now we begin to smile. He does it
again and we start to laugh.
Once more and now we are belly laughing,
rolling around the grass. There we are, two Indians
and a Westerner frolicking in the grass,
laughing and screaming
while Hooknose continues to emit
these most wonderful sounds.
Afterwards, we sit under the tree as before:
Hooknose on my left and Holy man on my right.
Only a short while ago I didn't even know these men existed
and now I feel more intimate with them than with anyone I've
ever known.
How unusual and yet it seems so right.
All of a sudden,
Hooknose stands in front of me, lifts his hand and very quickly
makes a zigzag movement, starting from the top of my head to
my stomach.
In that moment, I am frozen,
I can't move a muscle in my body, but my eyes are open and

I am conscious of everything.
In fact, more aware than ever.
I am sitting and watching them, feeling so much trust that even
if they stuck a knife into my belly
I wouldn't care.
Hooknose lifts my right hand,
places it on my forehead,
and in that moment something like an energy, rises
from the base of my spine, travels up my back
and explodes a little distance above the base of my head.
In this moment I leave my body.
I feel myself traveling to somewhere
I can't describe, where memory cannot travel. At some point I
feel in a totally new universe,
among the molecules, which are metallic green in a
blue/black space.
And now again, I'm somewhere where memory cannot travel.
For what seems an eternity I float in a void.
At last I open my eyes and the world returns.
I see they are looking at me, talking to me,
but what is this strange language they're using?
And why are their eyes looking above my head?
'Mmm', they must be talking to a higher self within me.
It appears they are giving instructions
or possibly there is a conference happening.
Whatever it is, it is beyond my understanding. And that is an

understatement. I feel at the level of consciousness of a dog
compared to a human.

We continue to sit. I watch them play a game together.
One gives a object to the other,
they argue about it and then the other returns it.
Again, they repeat the play.
I think to myself, 'I want to play this game.'
I take money from my bag and place it in front of them. Holy
man looks at me and says 'More!'
I feel resistance for a second,
but something within lets go
and overwhelms me. I dump my entire bag
containing all my money,
tickets and passport in front of them.
In this instant my heart bursts forth in love
as never before.
An avalanche of blissful tears cascades down my cheeks
and I collapse into the laps of these two very strange
and wonderful men.
I never knew that giving could be so beautiful.
Holy man says, 'Passport? Need? You take!'
Then he says, 'Ticket? Money? Need? You take!'
In a way I knew they would return everything
but that didn't stop me from feeling
very grateful when they did.
We continue to sit and while watching them,

*I start to wonder about what I will do? Should I drop my life
and be with them?
The thought of wandering around India with no money scares
me.
Then I remember I promised myself
that no matter what would happen,
I would catch the evening train to Pakistan.
So, without saying a word, I stand up and leave.
Looking back, I see they are staring at me with blank faces.
I have no idea what they are feeling
about my departure.
And walking away I notice I don't know where my body is - I
cannot see where it begins or ends and
any sort of notion about a body is absent; it is as if existing in
another dimension.
From somewhere above I look down and see this world.
I begin to hallucinate.
I see chariots drawn by white horses driven by Gods,
and railway tracks running across the sky.
Then a vast kaleidoscope of quickly changing configurations,
constantly rearranging themselves;
taking one form then another.
I see the men exactly as if on a TV screen,
sitting still on the grass looking.
I know they are watching me and
they know I'm watching them.*

As if from a height, I become aware of my body and
realize I am in the middle of one
of the most crowded sections of the city.
'What am I going to do?
How will I ever get back to the hotel in this condition?'
Having no choice I allow my body to walk,
hoping it will return to the hotel.
The body starts to move - I watch.
The body stops for a traffic light - I watch.
The body crosses the street, turns a corner
and goes right into the hotel without an incidence
and still - I watch. And all at the same time,
I am floating from one dimension to another,
experiencing hallucinations.
When I arrive in my room I am not sure
how I managed to get there.
I was not in control of any of the action.
I flop onto the bed, looking at the ceiling for a while.
I wonder how am I going to pack my bags?
'I don't think it is possible.'
Lying, melting, sinking into depths of being, energy, sometimes
in the room, sometimes not, I begin to be aware there are people
in my room packing my bags. Without saying a word to anyone,
travelers in the hotel must have felt
something had happened to me
and knew I needed help to leave.

I feel such love for them.
'This is what compassion is then.'
These wonderful beings not only help me to pack
but bring me to a taxi and off I go to the railway station. Wait-
ing on the platform for my train,
the awe of the meeting of this afternoon
is still exploding my being into some glorious orgasmic moment
of now. Nothing can describe it.
The train pulls into the station, comes to a halt.
Endless crowds start rushing back and forth, in and out. For a
while I am lost in the bustling, chaotic movement. Finally the
train leaves and still I am on the platform,
unable to leave.
'How can I go when all this has happened to me?'
'I want to see those men again.'
'Tomorrow I will go look for them.'
I leave the station and return to the hotel.
Everyone is surprised to see me,
I mumble a few words and go straight to my room.
It is now the middle of the night. My body lies on the bed, but
my soul, my being, lies somewhere above my body.
I'm in an immense state of bliss.
Waves and waves of rushing bliss permeate my whole soul. In
some moments I leave, traveling somewhere,
talking with someone and each time I return,
I am not quite sure where I have been

or with whom I was speaking.
I am in awe of the immensity of this experience
and almost can't believe it is happening to me,
and that it is happening now.
Remaining in this state, I watch the night merge into dawn, and
dawn into morning.
After breakfast, I return to the park
and sit once again under the tree.
I wait for the men to arrive but they never do.
My waiting is not in vain, for it is a fine morning
and the birds are singing in the trees.
While I sit, all of the sudden I am surrounded by something so
incredibly beautiful, so encompassing,
I could swear another intelligence
other than my own is surrounding me.
'This is what they call God.' I reflect.
Merging in this all knowing, all caring, all loving
and all compassion, I feel myself dissolve within it,
losing all sense of the person I was before.
All problems, blocks and fears disappeared
in a split second.
The person who was before no longer exists.
Now I am consciousness submerged in this glory of beauty
and love, of knowledge and peace.
I feel and see with the totality of my being,
the oneness of all and the love of everything.

'This is Christ Consciousness.
This is the level that Christ reached.'
I am so totally at one with all.
This beauty called God I see
and feel in everything. I am its servant.
My devotion, my surrender is declared.
I am but the eyes of God.

I open my eyes and there is an Indian woman
bowing before me offering her crying baby for blessings.
I touch the baby and laughter happens - so much juice, so much
life,
so much energy pours out of me.

I feel as if I can gather the whole world around me
and embrace it. In love, with God around me,
I leave the park.
A man approaches me,
asks me to come with him into a nearby alleyway;
in love, I accept and follow him.
As we walk, a policeman comes,
stops the man, forces him away and
says to me, 'You must be more careful;
that man is very bad.'
Gratefulness overwhelms me,
the knowledge of the Supreme Being's protection

is real in my heart.

It is morning,
I am peace and love and it is infused into everything I see -
even the leather of the shoemaker I'm watching
is alive and sensitive.
I think, 'Shoemaker, treat your leather with more love:
your shoes will be better.'
So clear this is to me now; so true is this compassion.
I feel and sense we will enter soon into a new age,
where awareness of oneness, of love and compassion are truly
known to all.

Some days pass,
I sit in a train dashing towards Benares,
the countryside sweeps past me as gushes and gushes of divine
light keeps penetrating my awareness.
I realize 'I am' and this 'I am' is the Supreme,
the Absolute. I realize I am nothing
but an empty vessel to hold the glory of existence, of God.
I am but its servant.
In this deep communion with God, there is realization
and this is the real prayer.
Later that night, the glory comes again,
I melt in deep ecstatic communion with existence - every cell of
my being tingling with life,

and at the same moment an immense peace is present.
The whole night I remain aware, floating in bliss.
Towards the morning,
I remain lying, waiting
for the train whistle to signal the arrival in Benares.
As I do not hear it, I rise to inquire the time the train will
arrive. Upon doing this, the fellow passengers start shouting:
'He is awake! He's awake! Do you know we have been trying to
wake you for hours?
You just wouldn't budge.'
'What! How is it possible when I have been lying awake
with my eyes closed for most of the night?
Surely I would have heard you.'
This mystery is not to be solved,
for the train begins to slow down and enter Benares. Weaving
my way out of the train and station,
I engage a bicycle rickshaw to take me to
my friend's house.
This most extraordinary city unfolds slowly past me during the
one half hour ride.
I notice tension in my stomach,
it disturbs me and I wonder why it is there at all?
When I arrive, my friend
is having tea with his girlfriend.
Sprawling out on the floor, I tell them
everything that just happened to me.

Upon hearing my story, my friend screams,
'Oh, God! My God! It's black magic. You have been drugged.
You can't stay here. Your visa runs out in two days.'
On and on he persists until my resistance collapses.
I weep and weep and weep. Then, he drags me out
of the house and throws me into a rickshaw, takes me to the
station and puts me
back on the train to Delhi.
Exhausted, totally in a stupor, I lay on the top of
my bags the whole night.

In the morning, I awake refreshed, feeling full with life
and the presence of the divine.
At the Delhi station, a man approaches me,
tells me to go see a certain Guru he knows, but
I don't listen and go to my hotel.
The next day I'm on a train leaving India.

One month or so has passed. I'm in Kabul, Afghanistan wait-
ing for money to arrive.
This time was filled with all sorts of adventures
and misadventures, of telepathy and further realizations,
and coming back down into personality.
Slowly, slowly, I am living less in the new.
The feeling of the divine and what happened
is still present, but some of its purity seems to be gone. Yester-

day a voice entered my brain saying,
'Go to Poona! Go to Poona!'
I don't know what is there, but I sense a Guru calls me.
Perhaps I will live in a cave somewhere?
When money arrives, I go.

Chapter 4

THE
ORANGE
DREAM

Split Seconds are spontaneous. Previous experience or practice with spiritual matters is not required - they just happen.

Kundalini was unknown to me; I was not seeking it. I ate meat, smoked cigarettes and sometimes took drugs. My innocence concerning spiritual matters was probably to my advantage because there were no expectations. Why the ego returned after complete ego dissolution has always baffled me. I can only place it under divine will and will discuss it in a later chapter.

Money finally arrived for me in Kabul and immediately I left for India. In New Delhi, I met Holyman on the street once again. He brought me into an alleyway, asked me for money and I gave him what I could. I found myself leery and cautious, and not open for another explosion to happen. We talked for a while, I told him I will travel to Poona and he told me that he travels from one pilgrim place to another. At this point he asked me if I wanted to go with him again and I said "No." He smiled, laughed and started to float away and actually disappeared right before my very eyes.

It was very extraordinary and I was reminded of one of Carlos Castaneda's books where Don Juan opens a world and steps into it.

I instantly felt regret and had the strongest sense of missing something important. However, my ego had set in again and was determined not to let anything happen: I was going to Poona and that was what I would do.

I arrived in Poona by train, engaged a rickshaw at the station and instructed the driver to take me to an ashram. He took me to 17 Koregoan Park. When he let me out in front of a big main gate, I noticed people, both Western and Indian, walking around in orange robes. I walked into the ashram and approached what seems to be a main building. On the front porch, I asked a woman sitting behind a desk, "What's going here?" She looked up with a giant smile and said, "Why don't you stay and find out."

"Hmm, maybe I will," I answered.

That began a 15-year association with Bhagwan Shree Rajneesh who in later years was simply known as 'Osho'. The next day I attended my first discourse and for the first time saw Osho. My heart did not explode in love as it did with the Holymen in Delhi but I sensed some sort of silence around him. I thought 'Well, here is an important man.'

I was very impressed by his discourse on Patanjali's Yoga Sutras. On that day, he spoke specifically about the seven chakras. The way he described them left no doubt in me about his authenticity because nobody could speak in that way without having self-knowledge. In that two-hour discourse, he described almost every experience I had in those last two months.

Within three weeks I took sannyas. I decided to do this because I felt the need to work on my psychology. My enlightenment was slipping by me and I wanted to plug the leaks.

Something else - after being in Poona for two weeks, I simply had to have the mala and wear the orange clothes Osho asked his disciples to wear - it had become an obsession.

(I don't know why and at the time I didn't examine whether this desire was coming from my own source or from a sort of group hypnosis. There has been much speculation that Osho was using hypnotism on his disciples. I can confirm something like this happened to me even though there were no bad feelings regarding it.)

My sannyas initiation was very sweet, Osho was very loving with me and there was recognition between us.

Attending his private darshans, I felt his grace, his power and silence, and started to feel he was a great man.

Shortly after taking sannyas, Osho suggested for me to do therapy groups before I leave, because as he said, 'Much has to come out of you.'

Following his suggestion, I booked for a seven-day encounter group. In encounter, the group lives together in a confined space in which the participants interact exclusively with each other, sharing whatever feelings or thoughts that arise. There is no contact with the outside. The interaction can be both negative and positive. On the first day, the group leader suggested to us not to hold back and to be as total in our expressions as possible. I tried this and by the end of the third day, I found myself on the floor screaming and crying uncontrollably. All I felt was hate for my parents. I just wanted to die. Two months ago, I was in total Christ Consciousness and now all I could do was hate my parents. I felt terrible and did not want to live anymore. What happened with the Holy-men seemed so far away. There I was, back in the mud, identified with my mind and personality.

I became a sannyasin and immersed myself into sannyas life, which I found to be great. There was always a sense of magic in the air – a feeling anything can happen - and it usually did. So many beautiful people from all over the world were living here. And of course, there was Osho, the great-enlightened Master, helping us with our problems and creating a vast Buddhafield. His discourses were brilliant and we flew with him into the unknown every day, feeling like we were doing something unique and wonderful. I became totally involved in sannyas life, thinking it was the best thing happening in the world. Yet, there was a longing always for contentment and peace, which I only experienced momentarily with Osho.

I longed to return to the experience with the Holy men, but I could not get back to it no matter what I tried. I participated in groups, in therapy, in all aspects of the ashram life and after 15 years, came to the conclusion that therapy doesn't give any real results other than the need for more therapy. I forgot my own experience that in a split second I could go simply beyond the mind and its problems.

Living in Osho's Buddhafield gave me the opportunity to live out many desires. So many people were ready to jump and we jumped freely into many interesting situations. In the areas of relationship and sexual exploration, we would say we were living seven times faster than normal life. We tried not to hold back any expressions of feelings and thoughts. Osho always suggested that all we need is to be total in our actions and this would lead to happiness and fulfillment. Under Osho's guidance we thought we were going into these matter consciously.

The problem I found was that no matter how total I was, it was never enough or another person was more total. It left me always with more discontentment. And the desires never ended. There was always the next woman or the next power trip. Again, discontentment was created. By the time Osho died, the ecstasy of sannyas was gone and mostly I was in agony. Even though I lived out many desires, participated in the collective desire to built a commune and create a buddhafield, explored my deep unconscious psychologically and emotionally, doing every type of therapy, I was even more unhappy.

It was at this time the desire to find a different direction, a new teaching, arose in me.

Many seekers gathered around Osho who lived in the vicinity of the ashram. He attracted many people from different spiritual practices and quite an esoteric scene developed.

One afternoon I visited with my girlfriend a woman Tarot reader. We spent the night in her house and woke up in the morning to the next Split Second.

SPLIT SECOND 4

One morning I woke to the sounds of a woman
giving a Tarot reading.
Often, I watched her give readings,
always the cards looked significant and beautiful
but never did they have real meaning for me.
That morning, to my complete surprise and astonishment,
as I looked at the cards, I understood them completely -
as if waking up one morning
and finding yourself able to speak and understand
another language.
A transmission of knowledge occurred with no effort
or study.
the next week the woman dissappeared
and was not heard from for years.
And I ... became a reader of cards.

Chapter 5

COLLECTION

OF

MADNESS

Consciousness is very mysterious and paradoxical. What is perceived through our senses as real is usually not. Truth cannot be known for it is beyond and bigger than the limited perceptions of mind and imagination.

We limit ourselves with our beliefs and concepts because the mind wants the world to be fixed and predictable so it can feel secure. It knows it cannot exist in the unknown.

When a person first enters into the mystery, usually fear arises. A person can ascertain their experience is genuine when fear is accompanied with it.

It appears to our senses that only this three-dimensional world exists; however, existence is multidimensional. There is a dimension of time, which everyone knows, and there is dimension of 'no time', which is only known to a few. Split Seconds are a entry into 'no time'.

Mostly everyone believes mind is the individual mind. In truth, there is no individual mind. There is just mind and it is universal. The feeling of possessing an individual mind is only apparent - mind is collective and impersonal.

There is an aspect of mind called the Collective Unconscious (CU). The CU can be compared to a vast sea of thoughts, concepts and memories, which apparently exist in consciousness. The CU exists because of our persistent belief in its reality. Each one of us is continuously producing and emitting thoughts. Conversely we constantly absorb thoughts from the collective thought atmosphere.

Each nation, each religion has it own milieu. For example, if I meditate in a Christian place, I visualize Christ; in a Buddhist area, the Buddha; in a Hindu area, Krishna, Rama or Shiva. In each instance I touch the particular thought constructs and memories of that particular belief. This is true also with different societies and groups. Have you noticed how we become like people and groups we associate with?

Some years ago I returned to Poona to participate in a ten-day group. One afternoon we experimented with a third eye meditation with around a hundred people. Special vibrational music was played as we linked together physically and synchronized our breaths. After a hour, the energy became strong and intense. Suddenly we were told to stop and link into the third eye. When I did this, I left my body and plunged deep in the Collective Unconscious and the next Split Second.

SPLIT SECOND 5

Traveling the Collective Unconscious one day,
I came upon a cave entrance with
huge double-arched doors.
The massive doors swung open.
Before me
was a small tunnel-like cave, which led out
into a huge space as far as the eye can see.
Contained in that space were
endless huge square pits,
one after the other. Inside the pits were rows and rows
of little opaque white oval forms, each having a head.
The forms were very neatly placed together,
each one moving slightly up and down.
Once in awhile one left, flying away.
Sometimes one returned.
I watched this for a very long time.

I began to wonder if these were disembodied souls.
After a while I was in another realm.
The sky was blue-black like night,
Stars were shining and I could see a bat flying
across a very bright full Moon.
To my surprise, along came a witch
wearing a long pointed hat, riding a broomstick.
Suddenly, I entered a room and
there stood Dracula
and then Frankenstein, followed by every monster
I've ever seen, imagined or dreamt of in my life.
Everyone looked as they were supposed to look,
as they did in the movies.
At last, I was together with the Devil,
he looked so sinister with his red cape, pointed beard
and slanted eyes. He began cutting me up,
throwing me into the fire,
and proceeded with every known torture,
to continuously kill me in every way again and again.
I began to laugh, really laugh; it was such a joke.
In that moment, I saw that it was all papier-mâché,
not real, but just an illusion.
All our monsters, our demons, our fears,
were mental constructs,
created by our collective mind.
I understood Jung's universal symbols

and knew why the monsters looked exactly
as our culture imagined them to be.
The fear of death, of devils disappeared.
I found myself above this now,
in a place I did not know.
I looked down and saw a battle being fought.
Perhaps it was World War II.
Looking further I saw the American Civil War.
I realized that I was traveling into the past.
With this knowledge I knew I could turn around
and go into the future.
I choose not do this.
I returned and opened my eyes.

Appendage

There is a very interesting truth that whatever we believe becomes real. If we believe in hell, devils and demons will haunt us even after death. As soon as we see this mind stuff is illusion, a dream, these devils immediately disappear and no longer does this realm have a hold on us. It is a very sad state of the world that 99.99% of the population believes the Collective Unconscious is real. We are all lost in this dream and are suffering for it.

One aspect of enlightenment is waking up to the illusions of mind.

Chapter 6

PAPAJI

In June '91, I received a fax in Poona informing me that a friend of mine, who was recently with a Master in the Himalayas, claimed to have become enlightened in just two weeks. My first response was of disbelief. It was more likely my friend was freaked out. Shortly afterwards, I returned to Germany for a much needed rest from the hardships of India. I dreamt of spending a nice relaxing summer in Ibiza. As it happens, the subject of my friend ensued while visiting friends in Amsterdam and we decided to give him a call. While speaking to him, it began to dawn on me that his story might be true. 'Well, why not', I thought. 'We all have been working hard for years and it was about time someone did it.'

Later, while browsing in a bookshop, I came across a book written by a disciple of this Master in which the disciple recounted his time and experiences with that Master and it sounded very nice. But the last thing I wanted to do at that time was to return to India and my ticket to Ibiza was already purchased. However, when it approached the time to leave, I called up my travel agent, canceled the Ibiza ticket and ordered one for India. I had to go even if there was only five percent chance of enlightenment happening. I had to go and see for myself; after all, what was this life about but to seek Enlightenment?

So, on a beautiful summer day in July '91, I departed Germany and flew to Lucknow, India to meet H.W.L. Poonjaji. Little did I know this was to begin the most beautiful and rewarding time of my life.

I contacted Poonjaji's son in Lucknow. He gave me directions to Poonjaji's house and told me to arrive there the next morning at 9 am.

Poonjaji's house was located in an outer district of Lucknow, not far from a forest area, called Indira Nagar. Indira Nagar was not esthetically beautiful and it appeared to me the whole of Lucknow was poor. I found the house to be small and simple, built of concrete, which was typical for houses of the area. Arriving that morning, I entered a small living room where Poonjaji conducted his meetings.

I must have been late for everyone was already seated. In the front of the room, on a dais, a Indian man sat with his eyes closed. There were eight people present and all were westerners.

So without any introductions I sat down and closed my eyes. Immediately I felt a movement of energy within me that continued again and again, wave upon wave - cascades of energy ran up and down my body. Among those waves, I sensed my mind coming and going and by the end of the meeting, a new sense of quietness was present. I made no physical contact with Poonjaji since I could hardly sit up.

People asked questions and I heard him answer something about desires and of allowing existence to come into one. During that first meeting I simply went beyond any expectations I had of Poonjaji. He was real and was able to share his Shakti (divine energy).

The next morning I arrived with some anticipation. Would the same happen again? I did not have to worry because immediately upon sitting I felt waves of energy coming into me and at the same time I was aware of something in my heart melting. I made contact with Papaji and we had a good talk. I asked him about making effort because he talked about it. He answered: 'I should not make any effort. I should drop all my ideas, notions and concepts, and just be quiet.' It was difficult to relate or believe what he said to me, but the contact and energy was so immense and that was enough - it felt so good to be back in this energy.

I arrived the next day feeling anxiety and pain, but when the meeting began, the energy started coming and my body began to shake and vibrated strongly. I opened my eyes and noticed Papaji, at the same time, opened his eyes. We looked at each other for what seemed eternity, although it was not easy because there was a strong urge to look away. However, I wanted him to look at me no matter what. After awhile, Papaji got up from the dais and left the room.

There began a half-hour tea break where prasad (offering) and chai (Indian Tea) were served. One of Papaji's caretakers came over to tell me that Papaji wanted to see me in his room.

Papaji's room consisted of two small cots, one table and a refrigerator - very simple and small. When I entered the room, Papaji was sitting on his bed. He looked up and smiled. The love and happiness that emanated from him was so vast and intense I almost ran out of the room. Gathering my courage I sat across from him and he started telling me how great my energy was and how open I was. He said he watched my soul going into the beyond. To myself I thought, 'Well, I sensed that but what about the pain I was feeling?' (Later I understood that I focused on pain rather than what was beyond it. There was beauty and love and more, yet I was concerned about a small aspect of mind called pain.)

Papaji asked me if I came here for a specific purpose because that was what he felt the first time he saw me. At first, I felt wishy-washy and shy about saying I came for enlightenment but something overcame me and I said in a strong and in a determined way, 'Yes, I came here for enlightenment!'

He started laughing and we hugged and hugged rolling around on the bed. He said, 'Yes, I always get people at the end never in the beginning and I work really fast.'

He told me enlightenment would happen in just a matter of a few days, perhaps seven days. We sat there feeling chummy. He asked me if there was anything I wanted to tell him. I told him the story of the two Holymen and afterwards he said, 'Yes, those men were very special.'

This confirmation was very important for me. The experience, up to that point, was so sacred I only told a few people over the years; it was good to have it to confirmed by a Master.

Going home I had the feeling I should start to celebrate.

Those first meetings with Papaji were of great worth. He inspired my confidence to first allow freedom (divine nature) to be present, and then, to be able to live it. Even though freedom happened fifteen years ago, the mind told me I was not free and it was very difficult to even believe I could be free.

Each day satsang (spiritual meeting) reached deeper and deeper and became more and more silent.

I watched a real healing take place within. After years of doing chaotic breathing and rebirthing, breathing had become unnatural. As the days went by, I watched my breathing return to its quiet natural state.

I'll never forget the day when an immense peace and contentment arrived. It was as if I became peace.

Papaji's love was overwhelming. Sometimes he walked into the room and I felt lighting bolts of love striking me. At other times, balls of love would descend upon me.

One day in satsang, not feeling well, I stood at the back of the room, being miserable, just looking out the window, I felt the satsang energy affecting me and by the end of the satsang I was feeling good. Before leaving the room, Papaji came over to me and said, 'Feeling better?' and immediately left the room. I had a history of very negative spaces that were very difficult to overcome. Papaji's silence was so strong, that even with those heavy spaces, the veils lifted and the divine nature (freedom) was revealed.

Papaji was simply blowing me away. As the days went by, I began to realize the extent of his abilities to heal and silence the mind. The simple old loving man who appeared to us was the tip of the iceberg; underneath was a fully realized Gnani (Master Teacher), with a special talent to silence mind, open the heart and reveal truth once and for all.

Every satsang became a love affair of melting and merging, flying into the divine. Nothing was more important and enjoyable - I could not get enough of it.

The Master's help came sometimes with only a few words. In the past when I entered deeply into meditation it was very difficult afterwards to relate to people and this caused pain. I ask Papaji about that because it was happening again.

He answered,"Forget about people!"

You can't imagine how this simple little answer helped me. The desire for freedom was quite intense for it had become a question of life or death. In my room the next day, I understood his answer; the decision arose that if I never spoke to another person again nor walked out of this room, I would do it to win freedom. At this moment, I fell into a state of Samadhi and could not rise until the next day. The desire to relate to others, kept me from being with myself; the moment it dropped, I was left with Truth (divine nature). I discovered in a very real way that desires and mind trips were illusion and could disappear instantly once consciousness was present.

On another occasion, I arrived in satsang feeling my heart bursting with love but feeling fear as if I was on the edge of a cliff. I shared that with Papaji and he replied, "Why don't you make this cliff a sand dune, so it will be easy to jump off and you will not get hurt. Don't make a big deal out of it. This is just mind and it is an illusion."

In this split second, the fear disappeared and only love remained. I saw that fear was a creation of mind, not real. The love was present, happening, while mind created some dream about having to do something about it.

During my stay with Papaji, moments like this occurred again and again until one day the conviction of the illusion of mind was very apparent. Mind trips that devastated me for years I watched disappear over and over again in a split second in Papaji's presence.

When Papaji gave you his full attention in satsang, nothing compared to it. It was Rama himself manifesting and I will tell you of one instance. Seven days after Papaji told me I would be enlightened, I asked him, 'Papaji, I've been here now seven days and I'm still not enlightened.'

He replied in a very loving way something about if I went to the other shore I would be missed, so why go? As he looked at me and I at him, an immense vastness occurred, the separation I had been feeling disappeared and there we were together with no him or me present; only consciousness in consciousness. The energy levels were super intense but very ecstatic and blissful. It was a song of our hearts beating together.

Later in my room, energy vibrated again and something died within me. It was so overwhelming I had to lie down and once more I entered into a state of Samadhi for hours.

It was during this time satsang stopped being restricted to two hours in Papaji's house. I could be sitting in a restaurant or my room, when immense waves of bliss and divineness overwhelmed me. I began to feel and be like I was fifteen years ago in Delhi.

My life became very simple. After satsang I went home, sat in my room, unable to do anything but be in awe of the immensity of what was happening. I could only be with myself and never before did I feel such constant happiness and bliss.

After satsang one day, I went home and decided to sit the whole day. The next morning I woke up to the next Split Second.

SPLIT SECOND 6

In a moment after sleep, before awakening
as I became conscious, unveiling itself in front of me
was a vast incredibly bright emptiness.
No words came close to describe it.
It was brighter than 10,000 suns yet
I could look at it directly.
It is was virgin, so pure that even these
words seem impure.
It was absolutely untouched, never to be touched.
It was the beginning and the end.
The Source.
In the next moment I watched the mind switch on
like a fog rolling over the sun.
I saw and understood what was meant by Maya,
the illusory world of form.
The personality and desires were covering this purity,
this emptiness.
The world is of mind and it is just a dream.

Appendage

In satsang the next day, I related to Papaji what happened.

He replied, "Yes, that was the end-point of inquiry (looking for 'who you are')." Then giving me a strong look, he said, "Always remember this emptiness is your home, your origin and from there you always begin."

I began to appreciate during the next months, the importance of his statement. I found it to be a most helpful tool for dispelling adverse thoughts or emotions (tendencies) that might arise. In the past, if I was depressed, for example, I would not know how to come out of it. First, I thought it was real and I thought it belonged to me. Now I know it is not real and it is not my true Self. My home is my emptiness, the awareness. When depression arises now, I sit with myself, the emptiness, and watch the depression disappear. Before, depression could last months or years and now it can go away in minutes or even in a split second.

Over the subsequent years, I've watched this work on many aspects of my personality. When some tendency arises, I sit with myself, be quiet, stay in the present moment and watch the tendency disappear. Sometimes the waves are very strong, overpowering me. When this happens, I simply wait until it becomes less strong, knowing it will pass and is not I. I am the emptiness, the consciousness that is aware of the tendency and I remain committed to it and my desire for freedom regardless.

In this way, one is rooted in the Self.

One woman during the satsang said she had a dream the other night in which I became enlightened.

Papaji replied, 'Yes that is right, Bharat is enlightened.'

Chapter 7

THE OCEAN DISSOLVES INTO THE DEWDROP

The simplest way to discover Grace is to be in the presence of someone who lives in Grace; hence, the importance of being with a Master cannot be overemphasized.

After Grace has been discovered and consciousness breaks its identification with mind, the Master's work continues to help the devotee go into even deeper levels of truth and wisdom.

Moreover, the depths of sleep and ignorance are so strong that even after awakening, identification with mind and body persist. Old habits do die hard. By constantly maintaining the light of the devotee, the Master continues helping by showing the illusions of mind, until the devotee's wisdom, conviction and light are strong enough for his own inner master to operate.

After some months in satsang, melting and merging into consciousness that is Papaji, the last Split Second occurred.

SPLIT SECOND 7

While sitting with eyes closed one day,
mind became quiet, as time seemed to stand still.
I noticed the notion of
body disappeared and
I discovered I was a sea of Consciousness.
Somewhere contained within me,
Was something I once called body.
However, my containment was something so beyond that;
the body was something contained in me,
and not me in it.
And what was me?
I was consciousness aware it was in the ocean,
a vast sea of being-ness,
immersed in the source of the Self.
I could expand in many directions,
which were actually no direction,

because I was oneness, a unity.
So blissful this was; so ecstatic,
so healing and restful this was.
In this full wonderfulness, I floated for a while,
seeing that everything of our world did not matter,
was illusion and has never existed.
When the notion of body returned, I opened my eyes
and again the world seemed real.

Later, I wrote down these words.
There is a place where nothing exists.
This nothing is a something without form,
which is pure being,
full with the hum of existence.
In this: I am love, I am bliss.
In this: the world of form does not exist.
From this: I enter the world of form
and the world seems real.
So vast is this experience of being
these exist together in time - no time.

Appendage

In truth, nothing exists and nothing has ever existed. However, unless truly experienced and known, this cannot be conceived or even believed. The world of form, of time seems so real; in fact, more real than the real.

Who can deny we live in a universe of flux, of constantly changing internal moods and external conditions. One day we feel great and the next day terrible. Some days are right and other days are not. Wisdom lies in the knowledge this change is just apparent and illusionary. Somehow it goes on and yet it doesn't have much to do with our true selves.

We have become fixed on form and time; and therefore have become creatures of fear: afraid of death, of survival - not realizing or knowing we are something beyond this.

We are a incredible vastness.

We are existence itself.

Knowing this is to know where lies the gateway to end suffering.

When the breakthrough in consciousness happens, we go beyond the mind, into the ocean of Self, and instantly see the truth of what I am saying.

It is mentioned in *Split Second 7* how healing, restful and ecstatic it is to abide in Self.

After even a few seconds of abidance, we can feel totally refreshed and renewed, similar to a good night's rest. It is said we abide in the Self when we enter into dreamless sleep.

Abidance in Self is incomparable; it is far greater than anything we could ever know and from there, all healing takes place -to be in it is truly entering into God.

Bliss, ecstasy, well-being and peace are all attributes of Self, but we could expand and repeat these words over and over to infinity and still we would not reach the utmost depths of being.

Self is always, yet we feel separate and not nourished from it. It is as if sitting on top of a well with a closed lid, feeling very thirsty and desperate for water, looking everywhere else but where the water actually is.

So, what is the lid and how do we open it?

The lid is our ignorance, our persistent belief happiness lies somewhere outside our selves. We constantly look into the past to analyze and rectify our feelings of separation. We dream about some future perfection that will finally heal us. And all the time, we are standing right on the well, blind to the fact the water is so close.

To open the lid is to take a 180 degree turn within to look for the source of Self. The emphasis is on the 'here and now' as this is the direction where the Self abides.

In truth, we live in oneness and yet even oneness is not correct - zero is closer because it does not imply duality. We are existence itself and we are not separate from it. To accept anything less is cheating ourselves out of our birthright. The secret of happiness is to know non-duality; it is the only way out of the suffering of mind. In nothingness, there are no problems - only being and in this being lies everything we have always longed and searched for: bliss, love, truth, light and the most important, love of one's own Self.

Chapter 8

THE LION'S ROAR

Enlightenment is real and must manifest in a real way. It is not something far away, but here and now with us at this moment, with no criteria or requirements. It is what we are, only we don't recognize it.

Enlightenment must include everything within consciousness; and this means mind and behavior considered unenlightened. When someone lives in higher consciousness, all behavior is contained within it - there is not enlightened and unenlightened behavior.

People seek to achieve a particular state of evolvement and expect enlightened souls to act in a particular fashion according to their concepts of how an enlightened person should be. As this is not the case, many people become disillusioned when they are face to face with an enlightened being. The enlightened ones never meet the expectations we may have of them.

For example, you can walk into Papaji's house and he may be glued to the TV watching cricket or he may be chewing pan, an addictive substance. While he is watching TV or chewing pan, satsang is happening and people are helped because his behavior is included within his higher consciousness. For more than six years I've watched this. It is Papaji's grace that allowed us to see him in his totality and this has been a teaching in itself.

Osho, on the other hand, mostly showed his public face and many of his disciples gathered erroneous ideas of what an enlightened being is supposed to be like.

There are no models of enlightenment. How existence wants us to flower is unique, and there are no guidelines. For example, Osho conceived the idea of 'Zorba the Buddha'. This concept implies a enlightened being should be in the world like 'Zorba the Greek', tasting its nectar, and at same time, to be detached from the world like a Buddha. As good as this sounds, it is a concept and has limitations. One can be a Buddha without being a Zorba and it is just as valid. Thousands of Osho followers have tried and are trying to become 'Zorba the Buddha', with the result that many are misled into false notions rather than searching for their own true nature, which is unique for them.

Enlightenment is our natural state, which is very simple. It is so simple and so close we overlook it. It is a healing, a return home to this natural state – it is a love affair with one's own Self.

Enlightenment has been described and discussed in countless spiritual books. When we meet it face to face, we see the realness of it, not what is written in books. It is not about becoming a super centered, perfect, compassionate, and omnipotent being. It is about being with one's Self, and realizing 'who you are'. It is about waking up to illusions of mind and understanding the nature of samsara.

Lets us look at what is meant by this.

All four aspects of the above statement are actually one point. If we realize 'who we are'; we are being with our own self. In being with our own Self, we wake up to the illusions of mind. When we wake up to the illusions of mind, we understand the nature of Samsara. Therefore, the only task so to speak, is to inquire and find out 'Who am I?' From this everything follows and is revealed in its own way.

Knowing who we are is not an intellectual understanding - it is an existential happening of becoming consciously aware of our selves without the separation of observer and observed.

How to become aware of our natural state?

This can only happen through Grace – it is Grace that wakes us up, and to be in our original nature is to be in Grace. There are unknowable factors as well, for to wake and to stay awake requires something additional, something unknown. What that is, who can say?

A Sat-guru is a realized person who has the ability to help others awake. In his presence, if conditions are favorable, it is easier to become consciously aware of one's self. In this life, my meetings with Masters were the times when awakening occurred.

I strongly suggest finding a Master. The Master can show you truth even though it is up to Grace and the will of existence whether you take it. As much as we want ultimate perfection, it will not be obtained unless it is given.

Now, why does our true nature, our birthright, need to be given?

It is not that it is given, for we are that, but conscious recognition has to be given in one form or another. This form might be a spontaneous experience or a Master.

We are all lost in endless dreams. Our ignorance is so deep. It is almost impossible to come out of the dreams even with the constant grace and light of a Master. Our belief systems are so strong, so deeply rooted and close to us, it seems truly unbelievable we are something more than our beliefs. Awakening is waking up from this hypnotism. We awake from the dream of belief we are something that we are not.

At the same time, it is so simple. When illusions drop, one simply is, because truth is always present. We can't imagine there was ever a problem. We see always we have been in truth; only we were thinking we were not.

I am gratefully aware of the divine source of myself. Mind is still present; tendencies are still there; ego is still present and all are included within my being. Now, I know mind's illusions and I have the key to live in truth with my own Self. It is grace that brings me there and maintains the light when it is wavering.

The happening of enlightenment is not a happening yet something shifts deep within. It is something of a death and yet it is not that either. The change comes from somewhere beyond understanding, and is bigger than our limited perceptions.

It appears many people today jump further into depths of consciousness. Many are waking up and there are many Masters available. I have watched hundreds of people experience something beyond mind and personality.

Many wake up, abide in Self and watch mind return, having the feeling of losing their awakening. What is going on? Is the awakening an illusion? Is it possible to lose one's enlightenment?

The answer is a question of right understanding and attachment to desires. First, people confuse enlightenment with the experience of enlightenment. Enlightenment is the knowledge we are consciousness and nothing else. There are no objects of enlightenment and truth never changes. Our awareness, our consciousness, never changes. Everything else comes and goes. Love, bliss, clarity, peace and feelings of enlightenment come and go. What is left is consciousness and awareness of it.

Second, our attachment to the fulfillment of desires and our persistent belief this world is real, keeps us identified with the personality rather than remaining in the abidance of self. It is the rope that keeps us bound and pulls us back into mind, which gives the feeling of losing it.

When we first experience our own self, it is literally mind blowing. The gateways of heaven open for the first time and it is beyond words to describe it. At some point the mind returns and we feel we have lost it. This finding and losing continues to disturb until it becomes clear we are only consciousness and nothing else.

When the switch to stay with consciousness is made, bliss arises from the intrinsic nature of being with our own Self that never leaves. We are Brahma and Brahma is existence, consciousness and bliss. It is very obvious we exist and we are conscious but it is the bliss we are not aware of usually. The awareness of bliss happens almost as a reward when there is a commitment to living in consciousness.

Commitment to live in consciousness happens if mind is present or not.

We abide in consciousness whether engaging in tendencies or not.

How can it be any other way? It is a great wisdom to realize this.

A very few pure souls abide in Self without much movement into tendencies (desires). These are very great souls and we are lucky to meet such a person.

The majority of souls obtain enlightenment with mind. That is, there are still desires, which are being engaged. They are also desirable to meet; for in truth, there is no difference between these types. It is only in the apparent world of time it appears so.

Having right understanding is as important as the actual experience of awakening itself.

In Split Second 3, awakening occurred during the meeting with the Holymen in Delhi, yet I had no real understanding; in a way, I was like a chicken without a head, running here and there. When mind returned, I was at a loss about what it meant and hence the plunge back into ignorance.

The importance of being with a master after awakening is critical. It is a tightrope walk to stay awake. Any slight push can throw us off, back into ignorance. Mind is so tricky we mistake ignorance for truth and truth for ignorance.

The knowledge only consciousness exist, is the best aid to help from going astray. Mind can weave itself into the actual experience of awakening and many people go off track because of this - they don't stay purely with Self. This is one of the reasons why always there are so many weird spiritual trips going on.

We can be at peace, in communion with our own Self regardless of any manifestation of personality. The desire for perfection, which rises from mind, keeps us from our own Self and knowing our own eternal, never changing perfection.

We don't have to transcend anger or sex or to emanate unconditional love to be with our own Self. We can include all these aspects within consciousness.

Of course there can arise from Self, an urge for perfection to change some aspect of personality or to relieve some form of suffering. This divine urge can be followed while still being with our own Self. Only in this way can real change truly happen.

There is a commitment that happens with Truth. We commit ourselves to living the Self. I have seen many experience truth, emptiness and then choose to return to desires and experiences of life. It seems they are the first to scream they lost their enlightenment when suffering appears again. If we put our hands in the fire, we will get burnt. That is the nature of samsara.

If we look for fulfillment of desires, suffering is surely to occur. Some, who have this commitment, can also have desires and experiences of life and even get lost in them. However, commitment to Self, to freedom remains. There is no choice about this because there is no choice to have consciousness and to be in this dream. We cannot help waking up every day.

Discovering who we are is the only real action. All the rest is dream stuff, as permanent as sand castles in the sand. What happens within the dream is not so important because we are still in the dream no matter what. At the same time because we don't have control, attention to the dream-as-real must be made, for this creation is part of us and yet is beyond us.

If you could watch Papaji, you would notice how much attention he paid to the details of life.

The commitment to Self is the recognition: 'Yes, this is a dream; I know it and I know it is impermanent, and attachment to it leads to suffering.'

On the positive side, as Self becomes more and more our daily waking consciousness, we simply are it and are committed because to live it is superior to living in personality.

Enlightened beings go on with life, yet they know their happiness doesn't depend on external events. They know bliss is their natural state and they know how to sit in it. It is the most wonderful thing in the world to abide in our own Self; and for this, no change is needed; only the recognition of who we are.

www.ingramcontent.com/pod-product-compliance
Lightning Source LLC
Chambersburg PA
CBHW021219020426
42331CB00003B/379